W9-CKH-948

A pair of screech owls of the Southwest

HANCOCK HOUSE PUBLISHERS LTD.   Saanichton, B.C.

HANCOCK HOUSE PUBLISHERS LTD.   Saanichton, B.C.

OWLS by Tony Angell

Library of Congress Catalog Card Number 74-6005
ISBN 0-919654-25-8

COLOPHON

The text of this book was set in various sizes
of Linofilm Super-Quick Optima Medium and Bold.
The text paper is Mead Publishers' Black and White
Offset Enamel, 80 lb., dull finish.
The drawings are reproduced by offset lithography,
duotone process, 150-line screens with elliptical dot.
The book was manufactured at the University of
Washington, Department of Printing, with binding by
Lincoln and Allen, Portland, Oregon.

Designed by Audrey Meyer

Title page drawing: *Young dusky horned owl*

Published by:

HANCOCK HOUSE PUBLISHERS LTD.,
3215 Island View Road,
Saanichton, B.C., Canada.

To BRYONY MEGAN, GILIA NOËL, and NOËL GORDON

Pair of young saw-whet owls

A female saw-whet owl scans her hunting territory

Foreword

Anyone who knows birds knows that Tony Angell knows
birds. That is to say, he knows birds in life and actually
draws from live birds. His compositions are developed
from direct experience. It is this translation of life
experience that is art. It is the spark, the immediacy that
counts; and that is what Tony catches in these drawings.
He has the taste not to smother feeling with technique, as
those who can read the language of nature will
immediately see. The artist's job is to simplify, clarify, and
intensify his vision of the world, not further to complicate
it.

     This same feeling for nature, this same close-up
intimate and experiential contact with wildlife, runs
through the text. The consistency of the pictorial and
worded portions of this work confirms Tony Angell as a
naturalist-artist who achieves in both mediums the
translation of the power and excitement of life experience.

                  Don Richard Eckelberry

Young screech owl

Preface

When I was eight years old our family moved into an old home in Southern California that was only a half mile from the Los Angeles River. Along this stretch of water the banks had yet to be cemented for flood control and the adjacent marshes were filled with wildlife. I would go to the river with my boyhood chums or alone at every opportunity and felt no guilt about "cutting" classes at Rio Vista grammar school when there were lessons to be learned down at the marshes. When the river was "channelized" by a cement aqueduct the wildlife of course vanished and with it the chances for adventure. When this engineering project was finished, complete with a barbed-wire fence, I think that most of the children who lived along the river felt that they had lost a friend.

Fortunately, however, my grief was short lived for at this same time I met a new friend. At dusk in early summer I saw him glide across our yard and alight in the lower branches of a walnut tree. In a minute I was out of the house and looking up into the bright inquiring eyes of a screech owl. A friendship was struck and throughout the summer I would rendezvous with the little owl on a regular basis. I recall asking him assorted questions although not really expecting an answer. Who are you? Where have you been and where are you going? The questions were met with a curious nod and bobbing of his head.

Over the past twenty-five years, however, I have found many answers to questions that I have had about not only my little friend the screech owl but about the many owls here in North America. This book is indeed a sharing of those answers.

An owl is much more than a combination of facts and figures. The bird possesses a lovely physical form and a personality marked by strength and vitality. I have spoken only briefly of the scientific data relating to owls and have chosen rather to concentrate on portraying these birds as they are living in the natural communities for which they are so perfectly suited. My drawings are, with few exceptions, from living birds I have seen in the field or have had in our home. Likewise the narratives introducing each species are developed from experiences I have had with these owls of our continent.

In ordering the drawings and narratives I have grouped the owls of the same genus together. With the exception of the barn owl, which is of the family Tytonidae, all the owls of the book are from the family Strigidae.

For the reader who wishes to check particulars of individual owls with regard to range and habits or to pursue more detailed scientific treatment I have appended a short annotated bibliography.

Male screech owl

My thanks are given to Dr. Frank Richardson for his very constructive suggestions with regard to the text and the sharing of his ideas and diagrams on the asymmetry of the auditory canals of owls. Dr. Gordon Orians likewise carefully reviewed the text with me and has been helpful in refining its content.

I want to express my warm appreciation to Don Eckelberry who has over the past few years been of special help to me as I have shaped and directed my artistic talents.

And finally a special thanks to Noël my wife who has been a wellspring of inspiration and shares with me the joys of knowing the beauty of personality that characterizes this special family of birds.

Tony Angell

Contents

A male snowy owl descends from the night sky

Introduction:

THE OWLS OF NORTH AMERICA

Daylight gives way to dusk. Colors are lost in pools of darkness. Silhouettes are etched in moonlight. The animals of day retire and those of night emerge. This is the hour of the soft-winged owl.

Owls (order Strigiformes), as hunters of the twilight and night, fill nearly the same ecological niche that hawks occupy during the day. The processes of convergent evolution have shaped these birds from two separate orders into forms that are remarkably similiar in their habits and appearance. Although much has already been written on the life histories of owls, a brief general discussion here will provide a good starting point from which to study the drawings and descriptions of individual species.

The owl, like the hawk, possesses the predatory features of powerful taloned feet and hooked beak, but to hunt efficiently in the hours of little or no available light the bird must also have extraordinary visual and auditory powers. The owl's sensory plane is elevated to levels of perception that no human will ever know. A night-time forest which reveals little to a human observer is to the owl a community alive with moving forms and at times a chorus of chatterings, clicks, squeaks, and whines. The owls' capacity to see in hours of darkness is so great that they apparently see better in semidarkness than we can see during the daylight.

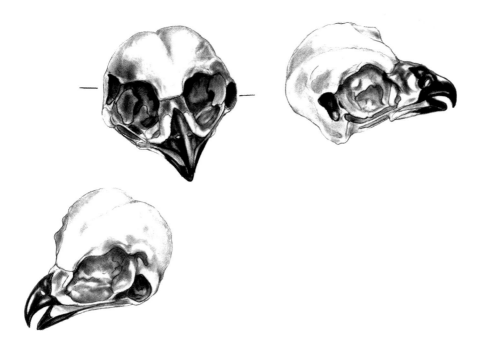

Views of a saw-whet owl skull showing the asymmetry of the external ear openings

When hunting, the owl will often depend upon a combination of visual, auditory, and tactile cues. Roger Payne found in his studies of the barn owl at the Cornell Laboratory of Ornithology that the bird actually requires high-frequency sounds for locating its prey in a totally dark room. The owl can perceive a frequency as great as 20,000 cycles per second compared to the 8,500 cycles per second that is the highest audible pitch for humans. In addition the barn owl has an aural disk of specialized feathers that serves as an external ear assisting the direction of sound waves to the auditory canal. In some owls these canal openings are arranged asymmetrically. Likewise the bony parts of the outer ear may be asymmetrical in their position on the owl's skull. Such asymmetry is an important factor in the location of a sound source when little or no light is present. When the owl has oriented its head so that it hears the sound with equal intensity in both ears, it is then facing the prey and is prepared to launch an accurate strike. The spread of the taloned toes reaching out from the owl's extended legs compensates for the very small margin of error that remains. Even the bristle feathers extending over the beak assist the owl in orienting its beak to a position where it can close on the prey. The far-sighted owl cannot focus distinctly on near objects so these tactile hairs are indispensable for employment of the beak while feeding on or subduing prey.

The taloned toes of a barn owl reach for a brown rat

Set into their full flat faces, the tubular-shaped eyes of owls are their most obvious sensory receptors, capable of concentrating and sensing all available light. In fact they are the dominant feature of the face. Unlike the eyes of hawks and eagles, the eyes of owls are largely external to the actual skull and are reinforced with bony sclerotic rings. (These skulls may indeed be very large for birds. One of a snowy owl examined was 2 5/8 inches across at its widest point, larger than an adult bald eagle skull also measured.) The retina of the owl's eye is covered with light-sensitive rod cells, the density of which is many times greater than in the human eye. The color-sensitive cone cells are not as abundant. This sensory capacity, coupled with the unusually large pupil that dilates to let light enter the eye, enables the owl to discern objects in dim light at levels that may be between one hundredth and one tenth of the minimal light intensity required for man to see objects.

The owl has binocular vision just as humans do. It is therefore able to make accurate judgments with regard to distance. Such judgments are critical when hunting. Unlike man, however, who can only move his head 180 degrees at most, the owl can compensate for its lack of peripheral vision by its ability to swivel its head some 270 degrees from left to right. A specialized set of muscles and fourteen neck vertebrae give owls the additional flexibility of movement.

In addition to their upper lids, used for blinking, and lower lids for closing in sleep, a transparent nictitating membrane sweeps across the cornea in a cleansing action while still permitting the bird to receive visual stimuli. On its reverse journey, the membrane cleans the under surfaces of the eyelids. It is safe to assume that this membrane also serves as supplemental protection to the eye when the bird is pursuing or subduing prey.

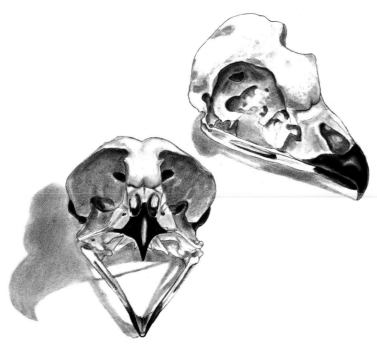

The skull of the great horned owl shows the large shallow sockets that accommodate the powerful eyes of the bird

*The fringed edges of the primary feathers of a screech owl
that permit the almost silent flight of the bird*

Once the owl launches in pursuit flight, its movement
is silenced by yet another feature of specialization.
Although the entire plumage of most owls is soft, the barbs
on the outer margins of the first few primary wing feathers
are particularly soft and fringelike. Air streaming over these
surfaces does not produce vibrations audible to the
animals or insects which the bird seeks as food. The broad
wings of most owls are flapped very slowly when
compared with other birds, permitting them to fly in a
leisurely manner without stalling. For an order of birds that
must do a good deal of maneuvering through forests or
over open country, this capacity for specialized flight is of
considerable importance.

Burrowing owl with lizard catch

When a bird or mammal disappears from a region we are sometimes hard-pressed for an explanation. Owls, to be sure, are disappearing owing to illegal shooting, trapping, and poisons that move in graduated amounts through the food chains and into their diets. Actually, the most serious assault upon their numbers is often the most subtle. Loss of habitat has resulted in a reduction of owl populations throughout North America. Millions of years of evolution have prepared the species to live in a particular environment and to feed on those mammals, birds, insects, and reptiles that are found there. If a particular environment is destroyed the bird is probably doomed. Its food source is gone and a different biotic community will have competing predators that are far better suited to hunt the prey species there.

Of the eighteen species of owls resident to North America, the greatest number are found in the northern portion of the country. British Columbia and Washington state, for example, have fifteen of the eighteen species either nesting or occurring regularly within their borders. It is interesting to note that as one moves north from the equator the number of owl species increases while there is a decrease in the number of hawk species. It is likely that the north country, with its seasons of long nights and semidarkness, is much more suitable to the nocturnal hunter than to the diurnal hunting hawk.

Each of the species of owls must work within a particular physical environment and prey predominantly upon those species of animals it is equipped to catch. In their hunting, owls are quick to catch sick, injured, or otherwise enfeebled animals. To succeed in this work they come in all sizes, from the diminutive elf owl, only five inches long, to the immense and fluffy great gray owl, which may measure up to thirty-three inches in length. The sexual dimorphism of owls can also help them exploit the various food sources in their environments. The smaller male owl has a slight edge over the female in his ability to maneuver in pursuit of small prey. The female on the other hand is slightly stronger and can handle the larger prey the male cannot take.

Two owls are especially interesting contrasts in their environmental dependency. A long-legged runner, the burrowing owl is physically suited to the open desert lands where it both flies and scurries over the ground in pursuit of small mammals, insects, and reptiles. It nests in the deep burrows dug by some larger animal. The spotted owl, on the other hand, seems short-legged by comparison and rarely has occasion to use his ambling walk. This bird requires a mature forest condition where a heavy canopy is available for nesting and roosting. Spotted owls hunt where the forest understory is open and generally unobstructed. Here these long-winged owls can fly freely.

A hunting spotted owl drops through an understory of branches

Although at the top of the food chain, owls must still defend against a variety of competitive predators including other owls. Young owls, in particular, must have a repertory of bluffing tactics. Almost classic is the owl's threat-display pose where the head is lowered and the wings and tail are fanned. The glaring eyes and bobbing head, the extended wings and fluffed feathers, make the owl appear to be much larger than it really is. If this display is not sufficiently threatening, the owl snaps its bill by pulling the lower mandible under the hook of the upper mandible. The distinct snapping sound draws quick attention to the powerful beak. The owl can hiss too if an enemy closes. Although the bird does not deliberately imitate the hisses of other animals, it seems likely that the sound would have a psychological effect on species that had learned to respect the similiar hisses of snakes and members of the cat family.

Still another behavior which assists the owl's survival is that of decoying a predator away from its young. Although this distraction display is common to other bird species, the long-eared owl for one has some unusual additions to the usual postures suggesting injury. I once observed an adult male long-eared first fly to the ground and then utter distress calls as a predator approached its nest. The calls were suggestive of an injured rabbit, and certainly enhanced its attractiveness as a possible meal for the intruder. Without extended study one cannot say that the bird learned to utter this particular cry as a complement to its other distraction displays. One can say, however, that the cries were successful in luring the animal away from the owl's nest.

A young screech owl fluffs his feathers, extends his wings, and threatens a curious Husky

Owls are also good at doing little or nothing in order to avoid detection. That is, their inconspicuous coloration provides an excellent camouflage when the bird is perched against its usual habitat. Some of the owls, such as the screech and the saw-whet, assume rigid upright postures when other animals approach their roosting place. The result is a beautiful blending with their surroundings.

Many owls begin their courtship and nesting much earlier than other birds and are actually on eggs well before winter snows have abated. Even though a great horned owl may be dusted with a layer of fresh snow during a blizzard, the bird's long fluffy feathers of chest and belly wrap the eggs in a blanket of warmth. Throughout this nesting season most owls will keep up an exchange of courtship and territorial calls that both secure the pair bond so necessary for the raising of young and discourage intruding owls of the same species from staying within the resident birds' hunting grounds.

Owls then are unique among birds. They possess an extraordinary capacity for sensory perception and are thereby permitted to work efficiently as nocturnal predatory species. Structurally, owls are perfectly prepared for the role of the hunter and each separate species may have additional specialization suitable for the environment it lives in. Their lives in nature are filled with dangers and competiton for survival, and it is rare indeed that the little screech owl reaches its old age of a dozen years or a great horned owl survives beyond twenty years. From an ecological point of view, however, these are important and full lives as owls play their role in the natural community.

Two young screech owls await their evening feeding

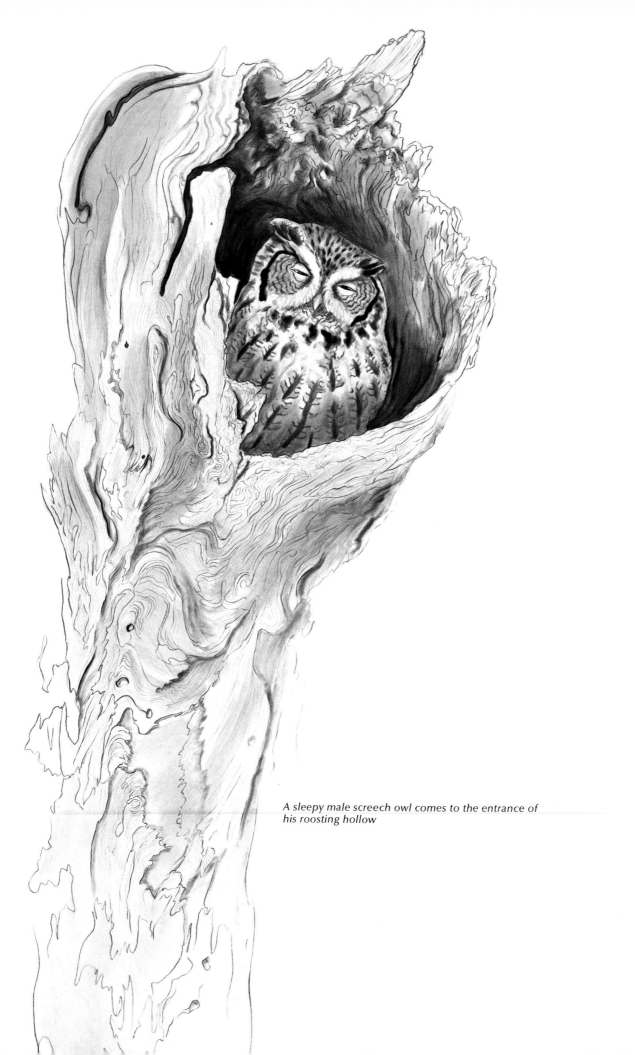

*A sleepy male screech owl comes to the entrance of
his roosting hollow*

SCREECH OWL
Otus asio

Length: 7 to 10 inches
Wingspread: 20 to 24 inches

Steller's jays break a mid-day hush with raspy scolding. The clamor is accentuated by the staccato cries of chickadees and kinglets. In another moment the chorus swells with calls of red-breasted nuthatches. All the birds dash from branch and trunk around an indifferent owl that only sought to take the warmth of the sun at the entrance to his roosting cavity. He sits benignly with heavy lids and feathers fluffed. The pose of indifference is misleading, for with the dusk the owl becomes a formidable hunter, and since he will sometimes take from their numbers, the smaller birds' scolding is, in fact, well deserved.

For the past several years we have enjoyed the songs and exploits of the Kennicott's screech owls which nest near our home north of Seattle, Washington. Their territorial and courtship songs begin late in the winter and carry through to mid-summer. As most of the calls are musical and pleasing to the human ear, to the other screech owls they must be extraordinarily communicative of moods and intentions. In greeting, food-begging, threatening, and courting, the screech owls reveal an assortment of hoots, whistles, and high-pitched cackles. Add to this variations in the call's pitch, rate, and intensity, and you have a considerable vocabulary for communication. The owl's posturing, motion, and feather erection are also important means of communicative signaling.

By permit from the federal fish and wildlife department we can keep injured owls in our home. One such owl is Dancing Bear, a very animated, one-winged screech owl. Whether on the top of a curtain or the back of a chair he is constantly striking new postures and uttering assorted sounds, many of which have communicative intent. Recently the male of the pair of neighborhood screech owls would arrive at the back of our home in the early morning hours and engage in a continuous dialogue of hoots, squeals, and bill-snapping with Dancing Bear. This scolding continued for nearly a month with the resident owl leaving exhausted for his roost hole just as the sun was rising.

One evening several weeks later the aviary within which our owl stays was visited by two young owls that had fledged from the nest along our creek. As far as the fledglings were concerned, any adult screech owl was worth a visit on the possibility that the older bird might provide a meal. The owlets employed their best begging postures and a "whinnying" call for more than half an hour. Dancing Bear remained indifferent until finally the resident birds arrived with food and the young owls pursued them into the woods.

The screech owl comes in red, brown, and gray color phases and a number of subspecies. It ranges throughout the forty-eight states into parts of Canada and down into Mexico and Baja California.

Male screech owl

A male whiskered owl furtively takes a bath

WHISKERED OWL

Otus trichopsis

Length: 6½ to 8 inches
Wingspread: 16 to 18 inches

Where spring rain has filled a shallow hollow on a sandstone shelf, a whiskered owl alights to bathe. His bathing duties are hurried. In these moments of dipping and shaking he senses that he is most vulnerable to the attacks of the other animals that hunt in the moonlit hours. After each immersion he pauses to look quickly about, searching for the signs of danger: a shadow, a footfall, or a looming form from above. With his soft feathers dampened he first walks from the pool and then shakes in a manner that sends a muscular ripple running from his head and neck down across his back to the end of his tail. A shower of watery beads is thrown from his body, and then he springs into the air to fly heavily to an open perch.

Sitting on a sycamore branch, he begins to fluff and preen, running the first few primary feathers on each wing and the outer feathers of his tail through his beak. He carefully cleans the scapular track of feathers running across his shoulders. Where his beak cannot reach he combs the feathers and scratches the skin with his foot. The preening ritual is completed nightly, for only with clean and unsoiled feathers can he fly well enough to catch those elusive insects and occasional small mammals upon which his life depends.

Although looking much like the common screech owl, the whiskered owl is smaller and is indeed a distinct species. It is resident in the Huachuca and Chiricahua mountains of Arizona, and extends its range through Mexico and into Guatemala.

A male whiskered owl pauses to preen his scapular feathers

A pair of flammulated owls rest together

FLAMMULATED OWL

Otus flammeolus

Length: 6 to 7 inches
Wingspread: 14 to 15 inches

In a cluster of alpine fir to one side of a Cascade trail, tired hikers finish their meal and prepare for sleep. Around them the trees tower into sparkling silence. At the edge of the campsite tiny animals track over the ground in hungry anticipation of the food morsels which humans always seem to leave. A soft and mellow hooting song is offered by a tiny owl winging to his distant mate. From somewhere up on the dark mountain an answer carries back.

Rarely seen and uncommon, the flammulated owl breeds in the high mountains of the West. This dark-eyed owl is the smallest of the "horned" owls, and its secretive manner enhances the cryptic quality that surrounds all owls. A color phase of the flammulated is, as the name suggests, rich in soft red-browns and cinnamon. The dark variegated patterns against cream and browns present a resplendent plumage.

This rare owl appears only infrequently in the Cascade ranges of southern British Columbia or in the high mountains of California and Arizona. It also occurs in those mountainous regions of Idaho and south through Colorado and New Mexico and parts of Texas. In Mexico its populations occur in the band of high mountains extending to Guatemala. Throughout its range the flammulated owl feeds almost exclusively on insects.

A male flammulated owl looks for a meal from the branches of a larch tree

A male great horned owl, with feathered "horns" erect, listens and watches

GREAT HORNED OWL
Bubo virginianus

Length: 18 to 25 inches
Wingspread: 49 to 57 inches

Rain gathers on the dense foliage only to fall again in thickened droplets to the forest floor. Below the canopy the bare arms of ancient cedars hang at their sides. A horned owl glides through the wet darkness in silence, and only the swaying of an extended limb reveals his arrival at a favorite hunting perch. He bobs his head from side to side, peering down onto an animal run where movement and sound have caught his attention. A young rabbit, catching some slight sound from above, instinctively holds his position. The hunter and the hunted are fastened by an invisible thread of awareness. Each senses the presence of the other yet neither perceives enough either to flee or to pursue. In the next moment a tiny footfall from another direction commands the owl's attention and the thread is broken. The bird flies into the night to follow this new sound and the rabbit dashes deep into the thicket.

Revered and feared, the great horned owl has long been the object of contemplation and the subject of scientific study. Still, few humans have actually seen this bird flying free. Although the throaty hoot of the horned owl has become almost symbolic of the wilderness, my first association with one member of the Northwest race, the dusky horned owl *(Bubo virginianus saturatus)*, was not in some deep woods, but on a freeway divider near Seattle. Here sat the great bird glaring defiantly at the evening rush of traffic, a large brown rat gripped in her talons.

The great horned owl ranges throughout the continent and concentrates its numbers wherever small mammals are also abundant and habitat is suitable for nesting. Coloration ranges from very dark browns and blacks to a northern race which is almost as light as some snowy owls. As with many birds, natural selection seems to match the birds' coloration with habitat, thus enhancing their chances for survival.

Few birds of prey employ their strength and aggressiveness with the intensity that this owl shows in defending its young and its territory. In such defense it will attack the human intruder without hesitation. With a fast silent glide, it hits and stuns, raking the head and arms of anyone who would climb to its nest. Such power should never be underestimated, for here is a bird of prey capable of killing (though not carrying) animals up to the size of porcupines and geese in both night and daylight hours.

In its pursuit of food, the great horned owl is an opportunist and sometimes takes animals that man also chooses to hunt or eat. Occasionally, it will take domestic poultry but as a rule only when its normal prey population has been depleted. Its benefits to man in checking the numbers of rodents (one nest area held the remains of 118 rats taken in a week's time) far outweigh its occasional predation on game birds.

Two young rabbits hold their positions when they sense the approach of a predator

Two young great horned owls await a meal

Six "attitudes" of a male great horned owl

A female snowy owl rests in the open upon a drift log

SNOWY OWL

Nyctea scandiaca

Length: 20 to 27 inches
Wingspread: 45 to 60 inches

A brooding storm moves shoreward. Winter waves surge at the rocky headlands and sweep over the open beaches. A wind sings harshly through the dune grasses and ripples over the milky white feathers of a snowy owl. The bird's flights southward from the Arctic Circle have traced shorelines and crossed open water. Now he will winter in Washington state, hunting small mammals and sometimes taking a sick or injured seabird. Throughout the winter the bird's white form will patrol the open coast and estuaries, standing out boldly against the sand and drift logs.

A bird of the Far North, the snowy owl migrates into southern Canada and the northern tier of states in small numbers every five to seven years. The migrations are stimulated by the shortage of their principal foods, lemmings and snowshoe hares. When these mammals experience a season of short food supply their reproduction rate is lowered. This decline in numbers of prey species forces the owls to move southward *en masse* in search of food. The already sparse migrating population is sometimes further depleted by a thoughtless gunner. Few birds survive to return to the tundra in the spring.

During these migrations many owls are weakened from lack of sustenance. The birds are competing for food with the resident predators and their hunting bounty is often small. Not only does the bird's weakened state permit the human to approach it closely, but the owl may never have learned to fear man. On a recent winter in Seattle a large female snowy spent a week amid the hillside homes taking her meals from a small but persistent colony of mountain beavers that had held out against the road beds and patios.

At peak migration periods the snowy will often congregate in open marshes, salt flats, and beaches. In the fall of 1973 the numbers were such that twenty-one birds were counted from a single viewpoint on Boundary Bay, British Columbia, and one report described ten birds feeding on a whale carcass near Ocean City, Washington. I have watched eight birds share a mile-long stretch of Pacific Northwest beach. They were uniformly spaced within the distance, and perched on whatever afforded the best vantage, whether a sand hillock or the top edge of a drift log. Their prey, when examined, consisted entirely of pelagic birds whose remains held evidence of oil damage to feathers and skin

Records show that this owl's prey ranges well beyond lemmings, hares, and sick or injured birds. Fast and agile in flight, the snowy owl can snatch crows from the air and fish from the water. When it is nesting the snowy is most dependent upon the lemming; when these small mammals are in decline the owls may not nest at all. On the other hand, when the animal is abundant the owls may have more than a dozen owlets ranging in age from several weeks to only a few days old. When the adults feed their young, they often retrieve food from a cache of small mammals.

A family of young snowy owls of varying ages

A female snowy owl pauses from her preening

A migrating hawk owl alights on a snag

HAWK OWL

Surnia ulula

Length: 14½ to 17½ inches
Wingspread: 31 to 33 inches

It is November and a morning of meadow mists rising. On the stubble and frayed stems remnant spider webs are still beaded with ice. Warmed by the fresh sun a migrant comes to the east Cascade country.

Abroad in daylight, a hawk owl alights in an old solitary snag. His silhouette and manner are not typical of owls. Sleek and tapered of body, from a distance he appears to be a medium-sized hawk with tail flicking nervously. As he crouches over the branch, only the heavy feathering of the rounded head suggests that this is an owl.

He peers down into the grasses that had flourished on the now dry and open ground of what had once been a beaver pond. The thick mat in mid-autumn is stiffened by the frozen dew. Beneath the mat meadow voles race back and forth through their network of tunnels. Suddenly, a quivering of a single taut blade and a high-pitched squeak trigger a response in the owl, and he dives to pin a small animal amid the grasses. Just as quickly, a bold raven sallies out over the open ground, "croaking" as he wheels above the hunter. The hawk owl instinctively opens and drops his wings to cover his prey and to resist any attempt by the raven to pirate his catch.

This circumpolar species is found in the top portion of the continent and only rarely migrates into the northernmost of the forty-eight states. Such migrations are, like those of other northern owls, motivated by the scarcity of prey species in the hawk owl's usual hunting territories.

A hawk owl pins a meadow vole to the ground

41

An Oregon junco escapes a hunting pygmy owl

PYGMY OWL

Glaucidium gnoma

Length: 6½ to 7½ inches
Wingspread: 14½ to 15½ inches

A winter wind twists and knots the meadow grasses into a whirligig pattern of browns and golds. Rain bites at the remnant leaves on the willows clustering along the swollen creek. Riding out the gale on a swaying branch, a hungry pygmy owl grips tightly, looking much like a plump hooked-beak sparrow. In another moment he is off in a direct, low-to-the-ground flight. Using a bushrow or a hillock for cover, he may surprise small flocks of juncos and pounce into their midst. Today, however, there are no surprises and he pulls up onto a distant fence post to scan the field with his bright yellow eyes. Throughout these cold months he will hunt in the lowlands. When spring comes, he will ascend to the heavily forested country to court his mate and raise young in some abandoned woodpecker cavity.

The pygmy owl (like the snowy, hawk, short-eared, and great gray owls) seems to do a good deal or all of its hunting in daylight. Still this tiny owl remains animated and active at all hours. For a week we had a pygmy owl living in our home and I was awakened late at night by his "whirring" flights as he moved from room to room. Snapping on a light I would usually find him on a curtain top, bobbing his head from side to side. On several occasions he would erect feathers atop his head just behind his brows. I could never quite determine what provoked this, but much to my amazement this supposedly "hornless" owl would face me again and again with his miniature horns in prominent view. The use of the feathered "horns" among owls for communicative display is thus far little understood by students of owls. This little owl, however, seemed to elevate his horns under conditions that would prompt a threat display.

In North America the range of the pygmy owl extends along the western edge of the continent from British Columbia down through the Rockies and out to the Pacific Coast into Mexico. Unlike the very similar ferruginous owl of the Southwest, which prefers the woody river bottoms, the pygmy owl usually remains in the coniferous and deciduous forests of the higher country.

A perched pygmy owl looks a bit like a plump, hooked-beak sparrow

Views of the pygmy owl

An adult male pygmy owl with tiny plumicorns elevated

A male ferruginous owl alights on a snag

FERRUGINOUS OWL

Glaucidium brasilianum

Length: 6½ to 7½ inches
Wingspread: 14½ to 15½ inches

Midway up the trunk of an old cottonwood in a cavity formed when a decayed branch was broken, a pair of ferruginous owls have nested. Here in the Salt River Canyon of Arizona this tiny species of owl has established a small territory for this nesting season. On a severed edge of the branch that still extends from the hollow, three fuzzy young owls have shuffled out to sleep in the fresh warmth of the early sun. When the mother owl flies in with a meal she first alights in a neighboring tree. Once satisfied that she is unobserved by any animal that might be a threat to her brood she flies to the cavity. The sleepy young immediately begin a rising clamor of begging, and the food, in this case a fluffy moth, is thrust down the nearest gaping mouth.

This early competition for food may well determine not only which birds will survive to the point of fledging, but also whether or not they will complete their first year of life. The most aggressive bird is the one that is most often fed, and when he leaves the nest he takes with him this aggressiveness and additional strength to apply to the hunting skills he must develop and test. In this nest the young owls are all about the same age for, unlike some owls, the ferruginous owl begins incubation only after the last egg is laid.

Like the whiskered owl, the ferruginous owl's range does not extend very far into North America. From the Rio Grande Valley in Texas and southern Arizona this tiny owl extends its population through Mexico, Central America, and South America as far as the southern tip of Chile.

A female ferruginous owl arrives at her nest entrance with a freshly caught moth for one of her three young

An elf owl in pursuit of a meal for her young

ELF OWL

Micrathene whitneyi

Length: 5¼ to 6¾ inches
Wingspread: 14¼ to 15¼ inches

A cool, fresh night descends on the spring desert. Amid the forest of saguaro the whine barks of foxes mix with the squeaking call-notes of elf owls.

A pitted-faced moon glows at the crest of a low hill sending shadows leaping from the angular cactus. A solitary moth, working over the faces of night-blooming plants, is suddenly snatched from the air by a tiny dark form that then wings straight away to a cavity in a nearby saguaro. His arrival is greeted with chirps and squeals of excitement, as an elf owl brings in the first of many evening meals for his family.

The saguaro cactus may well be an indispensable link in the chain of life for many desert-breeding birds, including the elf owl. Gilded flickers and Gila woodpeckers easily chisel holes in the pulpy bodies. The cavity may then serve successive generations of other woodpeckers, owls, and the starling as well. Although the elf owl does nest in hollows made in the willow and cottonwood trees along river bottoms, it is usually found in association with this lofty cactus. Indeed one might say that as the condition of the saguaro forest goes so go the breeding populations of desert birds that require it for nesting.

We are just beginning to learn how even subtle alterations of the habitat can affect the destiny of a species. When a single link in the species chain of life is broken, be it a source of food or a place to nest, the owl's survival may be in jeopardy.

Throughout its range the elf owl remains in the arid desert country that extends from the edges of Texas and Arizona down into parts of Mexico and Baja California.

Resting elf owl

49

A pair of burrowing owls guard the entrance to their nest

BURROWING OWL
Speotyto cunicularia

Length: 9 to 11 inches
Wingspread: 22 to 24 inches

In the rolling desert of the Columbia River plateau the afternoon sun of early summer brings the ground temperature to the mid-nineties. Nothing stirs in the heavy heat. At the mouth of an old badger den a pair of burrowing owls stand guard over their family, which is huddled in the cool recess below. When the heat subsides the birds will resume their hunting with one of the owls remaining close enough to the burrow to watch for intruders which might threaten the brood. A short distance from the entrance is a scattered pile of castings the adults have brought from the nest below ground. These pellets of undigestable bone, hair, and feathers are all that remain of the many meals that have nurtured the young birds.

Owls, as a rule, do not build nests, and when it comes to exploiting the available nesting habitat the abilities of the burrowing owl are particularly remarkable. To a large degree these birds nest in ground hollows usually dug by badgers, ground squirrels, or prairie dogs. Once the birds are in residence their quarters will, on occasion, be investigated by assorted digging mammals. To keep such species at bay the burrowing owl must employ a convincing repertoire of bluffing tactics that include threat postures and loud raspy vocalizations, one of which sounds very similar to the rattling of a rattlesnake.

Not long ago some friends brought me a burrowing owl. Like many birds that come my way this bird had made a tragic circuit. Originally he had been taken illegally from a nest in the desert country of eastern Washington. Little thought had been given to the dietary needs of a growing owl, and by the time my friends rescued the owlet his poorly nourished feathers were worn and ill formed. I placed him in a large enclosure complete with a burrow which he took to readily. If anyone unfamiliar approached he would dive from his perch to the ground and plunge headlong into his burrow. Looking into the hole one would see his bright eyes peeking around a corner in the short tunnel.

I once watched a roadrunner harass a male burrowing owl at the entrance to his nesting cavity. The larger roadrunner persisted in thrusting his beak at the owl from all directions, but the defender never gave ground nor did he enter the burrow. The roadrunner, after one of his lunges was followed by a charge from the bill-snapping owl, retired from the immediate area of the owl's nest. Whether this was a form of play as far as the road runner was concerned is hard to say, but the owl certainly took the attacks quite seriously.

By and large a bird of the western deserts and grass lands, the burrowing owl extends its range from southwestern Canada through the western and mid-western states and into Mexico. A small isolated population still holds out in southern Florida.

Pair of young burrowing owls

A great gray owl swoops down to snatch a young and unwary squirrel

GREAT GRAY OWL
Strix nebulosa

Length: 24 to 33 inches
Wingspread: 54 to 60 inches

In the half-light of early morning a young Douglas squirrel scampers awkwardly out onto a bridge of bare branches. Like an immense moth an owl descends silently from her hunting perch. In a moment she is upon the squirrel and then gone again through the trees, leaving only the swaying sprays of fir.

Throughout the taiga and in secret recesses of the Cascades and the Sierra Nevada, the great gray owl resides. In measurement of body size, this is the largest of our continental owls. The head of a large female may be up to twenty inches in circumference. It is not, however, nearly as heavy as the more muscular and powerful great horned owl and snowy owl. Despite her massive feathered exterior a female great gray will weigh little more than two pounds. Such feathering is necessary, however, in insulating the bird against the sub-zero temperatures that it is accustomed to hunting in.

Great gray owl

A great gray owl alights atop a young Douglas fir

Even the eyes of this owl seem too small for its large exterior body of feathers. Perhaps these small eyes restrict the extent to which it can hunt nocturnally, for much of the owl's activities are conducted in daylight or semidarkness..

In the winter of 1973-74 a great gray owl took up residence along a mountain meadow in the foothills of the North Cascades. On a January afternoon I moved away from the friends who were accompanying me and crisscrossed the grasses where elk had recently fed. I tried to appear unaggressive to the great bird that stared down at me from his perch in a small fir. When I stopped, only thirty feet away, and looked up, our eyes fixed on one another and then slowly he raised his great wings and glided down from his perch to fly directly to me. My first reaction was to raise my hand to permit him to land rather than to protect my face. His flight took him just over my head and, a moment before his feathered toes brushed the back of my hand, I had a full view of lemon-colored eyes set in the broad face. I whirled around and watched his gray form leave the open clearing and merge with the darkness of the woods.

When my friends asked what I thought had prompted the owl to fly to me, I had no answer. Thinking back, the picture of this lovely, fearless bird softly and swiftly gliding toward me is sharp and clear. To grope for an explanation might dissolve the beauty of that memory.

The full rounded face of an adult great gray owl

A sleeping spotted owl

SPOTTED OWL

Strix occidentalis

Length: 16 to 19 inches
Wingspread: 38 to 44 inches

In a valley where the rain forest grows to the edge of the Hoh River, a deep hooting carries through the night air. The sound flows over the trees on a warm wind and reaches a canyon wall where it is hushed by a rushing stream. Near the edge of a small pond a water shrew swims frantically for the cover at the shoreline. Its widening wake glitters in the night light. Before the swimmer can dive or reach the low bank, a shadow drops from the trees to glide over the water's face and pluck the tiny animal from the water. The spotted owl rises through the shaggy tree limbs to perch and swallow his meal in a single gulp.

The old owl has flown his territory for over ten years and knows well those parts of the forest where prey is likely to be found. His nocturnal flights have almost become habitual. He awakened this early spring evening and first regurgitated a pellet of undigestable remains of a meal from the previous night. After a stretch and a shake of his feathers he flew to the heights of a favorite old snag to call in challenge to any other owl that might trespass within his domain. Receiving no answer, he set forth on his accustomed hunting path. We humans would find his route well worn by his travels if we had some means to measure the use of this aerial space. In times of prey scarcity the old owl's awareness of where the small mammals occur in his territory give him the edge in surviving.

The spotted owl is actually the western counterpart of the barred owl. Hugging the coast ranges and Sierra Nevada, the spotted owl populations stretch from southwestern British Columbia through the far western states and then fan out into parts of Arizona, New Mexico, Baja California, and Mexico.

A sleepy spotted owl looks over her shoulder

An alert female spotted owl looks and listens for prey

A barred owl peers from the tree tops to the forest floor

BARRED OWL
Strix varia

Length: 17 to 22 inches
Wingspread: 40 to 48 inches

A country cemetery is now nearly lost in the tangled
advance of the hardwood forest. Old stone monuments
have dissolved like hard sugar lumps in the rains and
snows of past years. Saplings have rooted in the open
places that are no longer tended by devoted families. The
night sounds are muted until an old barred owl calls out
his declaration of territorial rights. His series of hoots are
bold and clear, carrying for several miles with the soft
breeze. He flaps from his roost and sets his glide to cross a
still open portion of the graveyard.

For ten years this bird has hunted and raised his young
here. To those humans who still occupy the distant farms
his call is symbolic of the mysteries that exist for them in
these Michigan woods. Many youngsters here know this
old owl by his call or fleeting silhouette against the distant
night sky. The bird has survived the many forces that would
claim him. Even man himself has tried to stalk him with
gun in hand but his wariness has made him unassailable.

Though in the near future his strength will surely ebb,
his memory of those places in his territory that are
productive of prey will keep him well fed. Perhaps he will
hunt these woods for a few more years and continue to
inspire those people who would walk to the edge of the
woods to listen and wonder.

The barred owl occurs as a breeding bird throughout
southern Canada as far west as the eastern edge of British
Columbia. It then extends its range down into all the
eastern states and as far west as parts of Washington,
Colorado, and Texas. In all cases these birds require
wooded groves in which to nest and hunt.

Three "attitudes" of a barred owl

A female long-eared owl watches an intruder over the
edge of her nest

LONG-EARED OWL
Asio otus

Length: 13 to 16 inches
Wingspread: 36 to 40 inches

A coyote pads rapidly along a line where peach-leafed willows grow in thick and shaggy forms. It is a morning in mid-May in the desert country of the Columbia River plateau. Along a trail the animal hunts; fledging birds will sometimes be caught. The coyote stops to smell and listen for any sign of prey. Above him, in an old magpie nest built only a few feet above the ground, a female long-eared owl broods her young. She holds her position with head low and feathers fluffed fully to the edges of the nest.

The animal yaps impatiently and leaps up along the trunk of the willow, trying to flush what might be in the nest. At the first leaping movement of the coyote, the owl's mate launches from a sentinel perch along the basalt cliff above the trees. He flies low, just over the animal, uttering a high-pitched scream that sounds much like the distress cry of a small mammal. The bird pitches to the ground forty yards beyond the nest and flaps his wings convulsively against a fallen tree and dry grasses. The cries, the slapping of the wings, and the awkward movements of the owl decoy the coyote from the nest. The animal races toward the struggling bird, but at the last moment, the owl flaps awkwardly out of reach to a point farther down the trail. Again the coyote pursues and again the bird flies beyond reach. In a few minutes both the coyote and the male owl are well beyond the nest and the brood of long-eared owls is secure.

The long-winged parent birds hunt the open country and shallow coulees for deer mice and wood rats. By the middle of June the young owls are out of the nest and roosting higher in the tree. By July the family has moved into the cliffs and the young owls are learning the skills of hunting.

Once while walking in the foothills of the Sierra Nevada I chanced upon a family of nine young long-eared owls. As I entered the grove of willow and cottonwood that composed their home ground they persisted in flying around their old nest tree as if tethered by some invisible thread. In a few weeks this allegiance to the home ground would be broken and the family unit dissolved.

Although the long-eared owl is more common in the West it does occur across the middle of the continent up into the East as far as Nova Scotia. Its western winter range extends southward into the arid mountains of northern Mexico.

Two "attitudes" of a male long-eared owl

*A daylight-hunting short-eared owl with a mouse she
has caught near a marsh*

SHORT-EARED OWL
Asio flammeus

Length: 14 to 17 inches
Wingspread: 38 to 42 inches

Below a coastal ridge a flood plain sprawls out to the edge of the sea where it meets an estuary. Long islets at the river's mouth deflect the water's ponderous flow into radiating currents. Here the shadows hurry across the earth and then suddenly dissolve as the clouds are shredded by high winds. A short-eared owl, dressed in colors of the winter marsh, glides gracefully just over the flat lands, chasing through the hidden paths of the wind.

Occupying the same ecological niche that the marsh hawk operates in during the day, the versatile short-eared owls may hunt in periods of both light and darkness. They are, however, usually restricted to the open meadows and marshes where, like the marsh hawk, they may crisscross the lands to search and research for prey. Although their breeding range is restricted to the northern half of the continent, their winter migrations carry them through the southern United States and into Mexico.

The short-eared owl begins incubation with the laying of her first egg. This results in asynchronous hatching. There may be an age difference of up to two weeks between the youngest and the oldest bird. This phenomenon can aid survival, for when food is scarce the older youngsters are able to weather the famine by feeding on their nestmates.

The birds often roost communally only to disperse to their respective territories during the hours of hunting. The value of such roosting habits can be revealed by the following incident. One fall my wife and I were walking with our Husky dog far out on the Ladner Delta in southern British Columbia. The dog raced out before us, going nowhere in particular but reveling in the fresh scents the breezes brought in. Suddenly, some twenty owls erupted *en masse* just in front of us. The dog was immediately thrown into total confusion and nearly somersaulted in his effort to track the birds flying off in all directions. When he finally regained some composure, the owls were well into the air and several fields removed from our party. The mass flushing of the birds seemed effective in confusing this potential predator just long enough to render him incapable of selecting and stalking any single bird.

Adult short-eared owl covering prey

Three ''attitudes'' of an immature short-eared owl

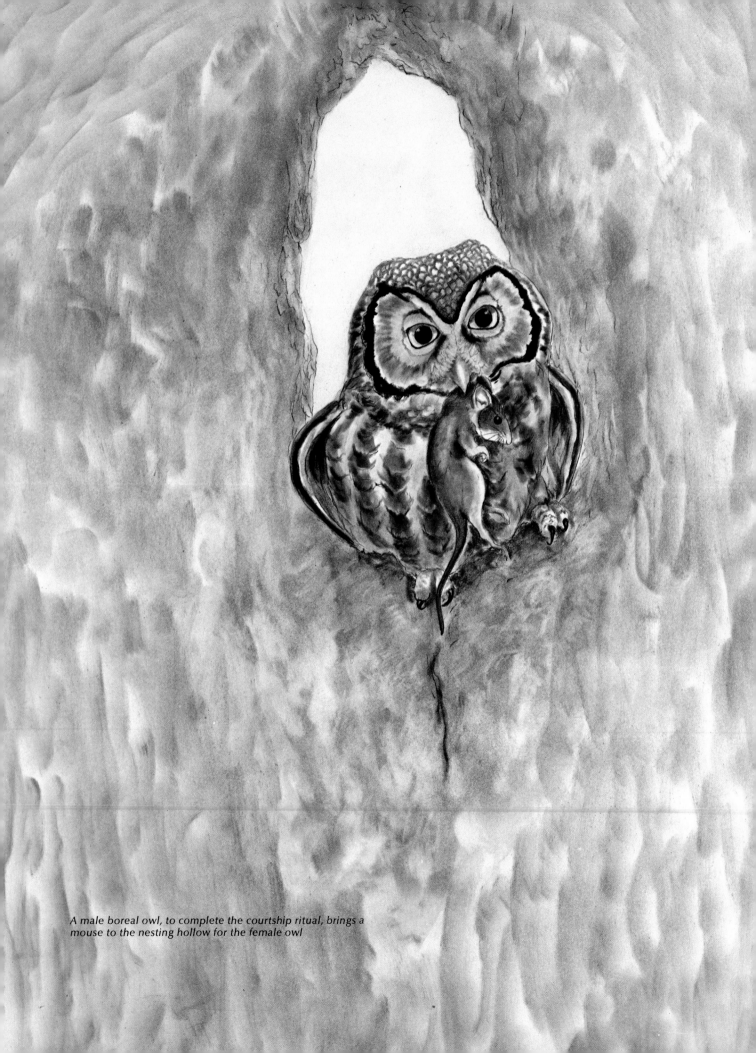

*A male boreal owl, to complete the courtship ritual, brings a
mouse to the nesting hollow for the female owl*

BOREAL OWL
Aegolius funereus

Length: 8 1/2 to 12 1/2 inches
Wingspread: 22 to 26 inches

Amid the vast expanse of northern British Columbia
wilderness, pileated woodpeckers have chipped and
gouged cavities across the faces of ancient trees. In one
such hollow, a male boreal owl places a freshly caught
mouse. Such a morsel becomes an offering to his mate as
he attempts to entice her to nest here in the abandoned
woodpecker cavity. Leaving the mouse he flies silently to a
high perch to sing in soft bell-like calls. The female flutters
out from cover to perch in the open and the male takes to
the air calling softly as he circles above her. He then flies to
the chosen cavity, enters, and just as quickly emerges
again. The ritual is repeated until at last the female flies to
the nest entrance. She accepts the gift of food, and with it
the site for nesting.

   In some winters the populations of prey species are
very low and this owl of the taiga moves into the northern
tier of states. Like the snowy owl, the boreal owls are often
innocent of the predatory ways of man and are easily
approached. Roosting close to the ground and looking
sleepy eyed from the night's travels, they are sometimes
caught by hand.

A startled female boreal owl

Female saw-whet owl

SAW-WHET OWL

Aegolius acadicus

Length: 6 1/2 to 8 inches
Wingspread: 16 to 20 inches

A bright moon washes all the forest in a fresh light. The barkless and bleached body of a dead maple suddenly comes alive at its midsection as brown feathered bodies pop forth from an old flicker cavity. They dance out over branches, flapping wings softly, and peering in fascination at the moonlit objects they encounter. A young family of saw-whet owls has assembled for a night of feeding.

The young birds display an intermediate color phase of dusky brown feathering over their faces, heads, and backs. Their underparts, brows, and moustaches are the color of fresh cream. By the end of the year they will complete their first moult and assume the plumage of an adult.

When the hunting parent owls feed the young they alight only long enough to deliver a meal and then push off to hunt again. This has been an exhausting spring for the mature birds. Beyond the normal courtship and mating both birds had to drive aggressive starlings from the nesting cavity and then compete with neighboring screech owls for the territorial rights to use the site.

Humans who remove old snags from the forest may unknowingly create an immediate shortage of owl nesting habitat. These are the trees suited to excavation by woodpeckers and the old cavity may soon become an owl nest. The mature forest composed of a mix of trees living and dead, old and new, is the special habitat required for the nesting of both the saw-whet and the screech owls.

These little owls breed across the northern middle of the continent as far north as Hudson's Bay. Their wintering range may carry them south into Georgia and in the west down into Mexico.

Three young saw-whet owls in immature plumage assemble for an evening's feeding

Two "attitudes" of a barn owl

BARN OWL

Tyto alba

Length: 15 to 20 inches
Wingspread: 43 to 47 inches

A plump brown rat slithers along the edge of a weathered barn. The peeping of poults draws it to the hen house. To reach the young birds the animal must cross an open stretch of yard, and as it does so a hunting barn owl launches silently from a roof top. She sets her silent glide to intersect with the rat's path. At impact both the rat and the owl roll in the heavy dust, but the piercing talons are quick to kill and the struggling ceases.

In a single nesting season, a family of barn owls may consume several hundred rats and mice in addition to assorted insects. Only on occasion does this owl prey on other birds and when it does the catch is usually a starling or pigeon. The rodents caught might have wreaked great damage upon crops and poultry had their numbers gone unchecked. The cost to the farmer, without the owl, might have amounted to several thousand dollars in a single year.

Nesting in both city and rural environments, barn owls have easily adapted to man's presence. Their catholic tastes for nesting sites may place them in a hollow tree, a mine shaft, on a building beam, or a flat roof-top in the city. We humans are indeed fortunate that the owl's populations are spreading throughout the continent. By exploiting the habitat available to it in the city the barn owl feeds regularly on the rodents that flock to the food wastes and discards of a society.

Once, near Hollywood, California, I happened to fall asleep alongside a swimming pool while listening to the raspy shrieks of barn owls that had assembled in some eucalyptus trees nearby. A few hours later I was awakened by the sound of thrashing in the water of the pool. I got up and with a long-handled dip net fished out a sodden adult barn owl. How this bird got into the water is open to speculation but my feeling is that he fell victim to his territorial aggression. Looking in the water on this moonlit night he mistook his reflection for a rival owl and attacked it—with surprising results for the owl. I released the bird dry and well fed the following evening and although he was often heard he was never seen again in the vicinity of the pool.

Although the range of this owl seems to be extending northward it occurs for the most part in the southern portions of the continent. The barn owl breeds throughout the United States with the exception of most of the Rocky Mountain and adjacent states. Its numbers extend throughout Mexico.

A barn owl seizes a brown rat and is thrown over onto her back in the struggle

Bibliography

The following references are by no means exhaustive but rather represent various complementary approaches to the study of owls.

Austing, G. Ronald, and John B. Holt, Jr. *The World of the Great Horned Owl*. New York: J. B. Lippincott Co., 1966.
  A study for the general reader which traces the great horned owl's activities through its seasonal variations in a midwestern setting. The photographs, particularly those that catch the birds in their actions to and from their nest, are excellent.

Bent, Arthur Cleveland. *Life Histories of North American Birds of Prey, Part II* (1938). New York: Dover Publications, 1961.
  The classic reference for general descriptions of North American birds. Here the reader will find numerous subspecies of owls described as to nesting habits, eggs, young, plumages, food, behavior, voice, and range. The accounts of the birds are often laced with the personal experiences of observers from all over the country, many of whom were the prominent ornithologists of the late nineteenth century.

Burton, John A., ed. *Owls of the World: Their Evolution, Structure, and Ecology*. New York: E. P. Dutton and Company, 1973.
  Very helpful reference for those interested in world-wide distribution of owls. Interesting discussion on the evolution of the owl as an avian order of birds with consideration of the conservation of owls and owl voices.

Cameron, Angus, and Peter Parnell. *The Night Watchers*. New York: Four Winds Press, 1971.
  North American owls are pictured in pen and ink by the artist, Parnell, with emphasis on the myth, mysticism, and folklore that surround them.

Craighead, John J., and Frank C. Craighead, Jr. *Hawks, Owls, and Wildlife*. New York: Dover Publications, 1969.
  A carefully prepared scientific study of the predator-prey relationships of midwestern and western hawks and owls. The role of the owl's predation in a wildlife community is explored as are those forces which limit the populations of hawks and owls. The numerous tables quantify the authors' findings.

A male snowy owl looks down from his driftwood perch in search of prey

Payne, Roger S. "How the Barn Owl Locates Prey by
    Hearing," in *The Living Bird*. Ithaca, N.Y.: Laboratory
    of Ornithology, Cornell University, 1962.
        An excellent research article by a scientist,
    significant in that it provides detailed analysis and
    conclusions regarding one element of an owl's
    physical make up. It is typical of other carefully
    prepared articles on specific aspects of owl behavior
    and physiology that appear in other scientific journals
    such as *The Auk, The Condor,* and the *Wilson Bulletin,*
    to name a few.

Service, William. *Owl*. New York: Alfred A. Knopf, 1970.
        For those interested in tracing one family's
    association with an owl this book provides insight and
    entertainment. As many states and provinces prohibit
    the possession of protected species such as owls, this
    book offers a vicarious experience with an owl in
    someone else's home. It also helps to spare one the
    actual and often unexplainable end of such wild
    creatures—their death.

Sparks, John, and Tony Soper. *Owls: Their Natural and
    Unnatural History*. New York: Taplinger Publishing
    Co., 1970.
        An excellent general scientific review treating all
    aspects of the natural history of owls of both Europe
    and North America with an emphasis on the
    European. A short section treating man's attitudes
    toward owls as seen through his literature is a helpful
    introduction to an appreciation of owls in art.